From the pages of a Lover's Notebook.

Love, Friendship & Them

ZAHID IMAM

AF518983

BlueRose ONE .com
Stories Matter
NewDelhi • London

BLUEROSE PUBLISHERS
India | U.K.

For permissions requests or inquiries regarding this publication, please contact:

BLUEROSE PUBLISHERS
www.BlueRoseONE.com
info@bluerosepublishers.com
+91 8882 898 898
+4407342408967

ISBN: 978-93-7139-224-2

Cover Design: Aman Sharma
Typesetting: Pooja Sharma

First Edition: August 2025

Dedication

To those who have the courage to explore the wild terrain of the heart, and who bear the burden of silence and the ferocity of unsaid words.

To the seekers who dare to venture boldly toward what might be,

and to the dreamers who dare to linger on the outskirts of what was.

For every step you've taken,

every path you couldn't travel alone,

and for the bravery to discover poetry along the way,

this book is dedicated to you.

Lastly, *to you—*

Preface

Poetry is like a bridge which connects the words and silence, the feeling and expression, and it is the language of the soul.

While writing this book, "Love, Friendship & Them", I found myself traveling the paths of memory, grief, love, and rediscovery. These poems are the remains of those journeys—emotions that cried out for expression and phrases that would not go away, the events that once held significance.

This book is not just a compilation of poetry but it also offers a map of unexplored paths and what makes us unique. It shows that silence can sometimes speak louder than words, and the paths we once believed we would travel with others, we may have to traveling in them alone.

Every poem contains a part of me—and maybe of you as well. I hope you will find your own experiences within these pages. This book is a reminder that every journey has a purpose even if the path in the end divides us forever.

I appreciate you for letting me be a part of your journey. Even only briefly, let's travel these routes together through these pages.

With appreciation,

Zahid Imam

Acknowledgment

Love, Friendship & Them is more than just a collection of poems—it's a reflection of moments, memories, and emotions that have shaped me, my heart and my soul. This book would not exist without the presence of love, the strength of friendship, and the warmth of family in my life.

To my family—thank you for always being my first home.

To my friends—your laughter, loyalty, and companionship have been the light in both my brightest and darkest days.

To the one who've touched my heart in ways words can barely express—thank you for being "there." You've left echoes in these pages that will live on forever.

To every reader—I wish you may find pieces of your own story in these poems. Thank you for allowing my words to be part of your journey.

With love and gratitude,

Zahid Imam

Foreword

In a world that is too fast to catch our breath, poetry is a gentle pause—a place where feelings are expressed, and the heart is heard. "*Love, Friendship & Them*" is that pause. A collection of expressed feelings, emotions and memories that speak a timeless bond that shape who we are.

This book is a tribute to the people who stayed, to them who left, and all of those unforgettable moments in between. These poems are a whisper of the soul, an echo of love lost, of real friends as refuge, and of family as anchor.

As you page through these lines, you will perhaps encounter a line which reminds you of a person you once knew, a stanza which is like something you've always wanted to say yet never had, or a poem which is like home.

"*Love, Friendship & Them*" is not just my story—it's all of ours, written with heart. I invite you to enter these pages with an open heart and let these words find you wherever you are.

— *Zahid Imam*

Contents

Love is the poetry written not with words,

but with the beating of **two hearts**.

Love is a journey that isn't something you

are prepared for,

It just happens.

Just like any unexpected cold or fever,

It strikes anytime, anywhere,

to anyone, with anyone.

It's a journey, one that starts with the questions of uncertainty,

where you stand at the edge of everything you know,

and wonder if the steps you take are leading you anywhere or nowhere.

It's a place where happiness feels like a distant memory,

a place where shock is so familiar, you stop trying to understand it.

You start and stop believing in faith,

asking yourself if it's a dead-end or a miracle that will carry you through.

The "what ifs" become thoughts in your mind,
turning every decision into a heavy weight,
every possibility seeming like a dream that slips away before you can reach it.
But in the moments when you're about to collapse,
there's something—a glance, a quiet word, a hand offered in silence—
and it makes you wonder if maybe this is the part where you stop running.

When you fall, then find the strength to rise.

When you don't care, then learn the true cost of loyalty.

Not in grand gestures, but in the slow erosion of yourself for someone who was once a stranger.

Someone you never thought could leave a mark,

and yet their absence feels like an echo in your chest.

When hurt's too much to show,

Poetry bleeds the pain we know.

The First Glance

In a room full of whispers and faces unknown,
You stood like a secret the world had yet to show.
A spark in the silence, a breath in the air,
A gravity pulling my soul unaware.

The curve of your smile and the tilt of your head,
A thousand unwritten words quietly said.
In that one fleeting moment, the world held its place,
Time knelt to worship your gentle grace.

What magic resides in a glance so brief,
To awaken a heart with its bold, quiet thief.
For in that first meeting, my walls came undone.
You were unaware, but the story of us had already begun.

The Day We Met

The day we met, the stars bowed low.
The winds held their breath; the rivers flow slow.
The world leaned in close to the moment we shared,
Two souls meeting, completely unprepared.

I didn't know then what your smile would ignite,
The paths it would carve, the joy and the light.
But that day remains, like a flame burning clear,
The beginning of everything I ever held dear.

Love in Small Moments

It's not in the grand, nor the stars we ignite,
But the quietest moments feel most right.
The brush of your hand, the laugh that you hide,
The way you stay close when the world steps aside.

It's the way you remember the tea that I take,
The quiet "I'm here" in the smiles that you make.
Love doesn't shout; it quietly grows,
In the smallest of moments, it endlessly shows.

The Weight of a Touch

Your hand on my shoulder, palm on my cheek,
The language of love in gestures that speak.
The weight of your touch, so gentle, so kind,
Leaves a mark far deeper than words could define.

In the spaces between us, you bridge the divide.
Your touch is a tether where love does reside.
It's heavy with meaning, it's soft as a sigh,
A touch that stays when the world says goodbye.

An Undying Flame

Our love is a flame that no storm can douse,
A hearth in the dark, a light in our house.
Though winds may howl and waters may rise,
It burns ever steady beneath the vast skies.

Through trials and years, it only grows stronger,
A fire eternal that lasts even longer.
And should the world crumble and stars fade away,
Our flame will remain, forever to stay.

Rain is a Metaphor for Love

You're the rain that falls soft, a kiss from the skies,
A dance through the clouds, where the earth softly cries.
You're storms that awaken, fierce and alive,
And puddles that linger, where dreams still survive.

Rain nurtures, it heals, it washes away.
It drowns all the fears that keep love at bay.
So come as you are—be gentle, be wild,
For love, like the rain, is untamed and not styled.

A Home in Your Arms

Your arms are the place where the world fades away,
A refuge from chaos, where I long to stay.
The weight of the world disappears in your hold,
It's a comfort that's warmer than stories told.

In your arms, I've found a love so profound,
A shelter where peace and belonging abound.
No matter the storms or how far I may roam,
I'll always return, for your arms are my home.

A Love of Imperfections

It's not in perfection that love finds its way,
But in all the cracks where the light dares to play.
In flaws and in failures, in scars that we bare,
Love whispers, "I see you, and still, I care."

Your crooked smile, your unpolished grace,
Are the pieces of you I could never replace.
For love isn't perfect—it's messy and true,
And I love every imperfection in you.

The Fear of Losing You

I hold you closer, though I can't hold time,
Each ticking second feels almost a crime.
For what if tomorrow should steal you away,
And leave me with echoes of yesterday?

The fear of losing what feels so complete,
Makes every moment a bittersweet feat.
But even that fear makes my love burn bright—
To cherish each breath, each glance, each night.

The most painful part of love is its unpredictability.

No matter how much you care,

or how much you sacrifice,

how much you love them,

it feels like you are drifting away from them with each passing moment.

Sometimes its misfortune,

sometimes fate, sometimes someone,

and sometimes misunderstandings.

We once moved as one,

intertwined like branches in a storm,

our words like soft winds that carried each other's names.

But somewhere along the way,

the storm passed,

and the winds grew colder,

We became strangers, these hands don't hold her.

At first, I didn't notice the distance,
the way our laughter started to fall silent,
how our touch felt like a memory
instead of a promise.
But slowly and slightly,
I felt the space between us widen,
like the gap between the sky and the earth,
bridge too vast to prove it's worth.

We spoke less,

but the silences weren't empty,

They were filled with the weight of things unsaid,

with the unspoken truth we were afraid to face.

In the distance, I found fragments of myself,

I had forgotten in the closeness of you.

I began to listen to my own breath again,

to hear my own heart beat

without the echoes of you.

Love, I learned, is not just about the proximity.

It's about presence,

and we had both become ghosts in each other's lives.

In the space between us, I began to find my own shape,

to fill the quiet with the sound of my own voice,

to claim the space I had lost when I was tangled in you and your voice.

The love we had once shared

was like a garden,

beautiful but overgrown,

and the distance became the pruning knife,

that cut away the parts that no longer grew.

I stand on the edge of what we were,

looking back, but no longer reaching for what's gone,

because I know now, calm and true

I can love in the space I've carved into.

A Love that Fades

It didn't leave all at once, like a storm that departs,
But quietly unraveled thread by thread, from our hearts.
The words grew softer, the silences long.
The melody shifted and broke from our song.

The colors we painted began to decay,
Fading like twilight that steals light away,
The warmth of your touch turned cool on my skin.
A love once so vivid grew pale from within.

But even as echoes replace what was true,
There's beauty in knowing I once loved you,
For even a love that fades into air,
Still lingers in memories, tender and rare.

The Distance between Us

Mountains and oceans, they stand in the way,
But distance can't lessen what words cannot say.
I feel you in sunsets, in stars as they glow,
In the pull of the moon, in the rivers that flow.

Though miles may divide us and time keeps its pace,
In my heart, you've always been home, my safe place.
Distance is nothing to love's steady art—
It lives in the closeness of two beating hearts.

Love Across time

I have loved you in shadows of ages gone by,
In lifetimes where stars carved our names in the sky,
In the echoes of castles, in whispers of trees,
Our love has been carried by time's endless seas.

I have known your embrace in lives I forgot,
In debts I have, in battles I fought.
In the dance of the flames, in the hush of the rain,
I have searched for you, found you and lost you again.

Through centuries fleeting, our souls intervene.
Forever repeating, your heart beating with mine.
No matter the era, no matter the space,
I will find you again in eternity's grace.

Unspoken Confessions

There were words in my chest I could never let free.
A prison of silence, the lock was my plea.
Each glance was a whisper, each sigh was a scream,
Yet I drowned in the current of what I might mean.

If only you knew the storms I would weather,
To piece those unspoken confessions together.
But love left and silence soon turns into regret,
A shadow of words I can't ever forget.

Although our journey was long, in the end I realised how much more I had to tell you.

The Love of a Letter

Dearest, these words may never be read,
Yet here they linger, where they are fed.
With ink as my voice and paper my heart,
I pour out the love that we kept far apart.

Each line is a whisper, each word is a kiss,
A tapestry woven with dreams that I miss.
Though this letter may never touch your hands,
It carries my love through unmapped lands.

Eternal Echoes

You are the whisper in the night's quiet air,
The ghost of a touch that lingers unfair.
Though the years have pulled us apart like a tide,
Your memory stays as a flame deep inside.

Each echo of laughter, each shadowed embrace,
Leaves me chasing the fragments of your fading face.
Even time's cruel hand cannot erase,
The eternal echoes of your love's trace.

I may act like I'm over it, like I don't care,
but deep within me, there's still you.
Living in the corner of my heart
where no-one else can ever reach.

Hidden Love

My love for you hides where the shadows can't see,
In the quietest corners of what cannot be.
It blooms in the dark, unseen by the light,
A love that persists in the cover of night.

I trace every moment, a glance, a small smile,
And cherish each secret, if only awhile.
Though hidden, it thrives a fire untamed;
A love without witness, but never unnamed.

Seasons of Love

In spring, you arrived with a laugh like the breeze,
A whisper of blossoms that danced through the trees.
In summer, you stayed, as the days stretched so long,
With warmth in your eyes and a heart full of song.

By autumn, the colours began to decay,
And love, like the leaves, started drifting away.
Now winter is here, and I stand in the cold,
Remembering a love that will never grow old.

Once promised forever, is meant nothing now.

Love and Betrayal

Your hands once held mine, so steady, so sure,
A promise of love meant forever to endure.
But promises falter, and hearts can betray,
Love turns to ash when trust falls away.

The blade that you wielded cut deeper than lies,
I saw the betrayal reflected in your eyes.
Yet even in heartbreak, I can't seem to sever,
The part of my soul that will love you forever.

Eyes like Universe

Your eyes are not windows—they're galaxies wide.
A cosmos of wonder where mysteries hide.
In every small glance, there's a world I can see,
A lifetime of stories unfolding for me.

They hold constellations, both gentle and fierce,
A love that is tender, a gaze that can pierce.
In the depths of your eyes, I find something divine,
A universe vast, and somehow, it's mine.

Silent Connections

No words are spoken, yet I hear it all,
In the way your glance answers my call.
Your silence hums louder than symphonies play,
A language of love only hearts can convey.

Each pause is a promise, each look a refrain,
A connection that flows through joy and through pain.
We speak without sound, our souls intertwined,
A love that's unspoken, yet perfectly defined.

A Love That's Out of Reach

I see you in dreams, but you vanish at dawn,
A shadow I chase when the night has withdrawn.
You are there in my thoughts, yet so far to hold,
A love that feels close, yet remains so cold.

You're the star in the sky I can never attain,
A beauty so near, yet beyond my domain.
But even in distance, my heart does beseech,
For the chance to touch a love out of reach.

The Language of Love

Your love speaks in words I've never been taught,
In a dialect only my soul has caught.
It's the hush of your laugh, the pause in your stare,
The gentle reminders that you'll always care.

No dictionary could ever define,
The language of love that you've made mine.
It's a language of gestures, of silence, of fire,
A voice from the heart that lifts me higher.

The Echo of Laughter

Your laughter still echoes, though you are not near,
It dances like music, soft, crystal, and clear.
Each note is a memory, each sound a refrain,
A song of the moments we'll never regain.

But even in absence, it lingers in air,
A melody woven with love and with care.
Though time may have taken your presence away,
Your laughter remains, a light in my day.

Sometimes the journey continues.

Rebuilding Love

We stood in the ruins, our hearts turned to stone,
The echoes of love left us feeling alone.
But in the rubble, a seed still remained,
A hope that through cracks, love could be regained.

Brick by brick, we rebuild what was lost,
With patience, forgiveness, and weathering cost.
Though scars may remain, they tell a new story—
A love resurrected, resilient with glory.

The Quiet Love

It's not the love that shouts or demands,
But the one that holds softly, with gentle hands.
It's the warmth of a gaze, the peace in a sigh,
The love that just lingers, without asking why.

No fireworks blaze, no grand stage to see,
Just the steady heartbeats of you and me.
In the quiet of love, there's a truth that we find—
A bond that's enduring, unspoken, yet kind.

Star-Crossed Lovers

The stars wrote a tale of love and despair,
A bond that the heavens refused to declare,
Yet we loved through the tears, through fate's cruel design,
Defying the cosmos to make you mine.

Though the universe pulls, we cling to the thread,
A love that persists though the stars have said,
"This love is forbidden, it cannot remain",
Yet we burn brighter, defying the pain.

A Love Lost to Time

We once walked together, hand in hand,
Through moments eternal, like grains of sand.
But time is a thief, stealing days from our eyes,
Turning love into whispers and long, aching sighs.

I see your face now in the corners of dreams,
A love that has faded like sun-splintered beams.
Yet even as years pull us farther apart,
You'll always remain a home in my heart.

The Morning Light

When sunlight breaks through the curtain of night,
I see your face bathed in morning's soft light.
It glows with a warmth that the dawn can't contain.
A love so enduring, it quiets my pain.

The day may hold trials, the hours may fade,
But the morning reminds me of the love we've made.
With each golden ray, your beauty takes flight,
My heart wakes a new in the morning light.

The Soul's Reflection

In you, I see the parts of me,
That dance like waves upon the sea.
A mirror of truths I've tried to ignore,
But your love reveals, it opens the door.

Your soul reflects my heart's dream,
A light that shines through the darkest stream.
You are the answer, the truth I've pursued,
A reflection of love that feels completely renewed.

A Love that Changes You Forever

Your love is a wind that reshapes my shore,
It carries my soul to heights never before.
I was once a shadow, a fragment, a part,
But you filled the void and remade my heart.

With each word you speak, with each smile you give,
You've shown me a world where I truly live.
Your love has transformed me, from darkness to hue,
I am forever changed by the love I found in you.

The pain of one sided-love is something not everyone can handle.

More Than a Friend

You weren't just a friend, I gave you my trust,
My laughter, my secrets, my innocent rusts.
We danced through the storms, hand in hand in the rain,
And I believed you'd protect me from sorrow and pain.

But love wears a mask when it hides in disguise,
And I missed the truth swimming deep in your eyes.
You smiled like sunrise but burned like the sun,
By the time I saw clearly, the damage was already done.

You knew that I loved you, more than I said,
And still, you chose silence, leaving words hanging dead.
A dagger disguised as a warm-hearted touch,

You knew you were breaking what mattered too much.

You weren't just a chapter, you were the book,
Now torn at the edges, wherever I look.
A friend, a lover, a thief in the end,
You taught me how frail it is to depend.

But love still lingers, like ghosts in the air,
A whisper of "maybe" that shouldn't be there.
I'll carry the wound, but not the regret,
Some scars remind us, we never forget.

I searched for closure, but silence replied,
The ache of your absence too sharp to hide.
The truth took time, but now I comprehend,
And in the end, I realized – you were more than a friend.

A prison you cannot escape —

no matter how smart, no matter how tough.

This is the place where even the strongest fall,

where you will be the most vulnerable of all.

Love's Prisoner

In the middle of this night,
Thoughts rush in, as sharp as a knife,
Thoughts of your hollow love and lies,
Of every moment you spent with me in disguise.

I tried to flee from this memories grip,
No matter how far I slip,
No matter how hard I fight,
There's no escape from this endless night.

I surrender now to this prison's cruel bind,
Where the walls are built from what you left behind.
Where the guards are the moments, I once held
dear,
Now haunts me, my biggest fear.

Where the light is a flicker of time we shared,

A glow that fades away, which I no longer cared.

In the pitch-black corner of this cell, my heart does stay,

Trapped in this prison, with no hope of day.

I put my armour on to meet you, knowing my fate.

Yet your words were so sharp, they pierced right through my armour — and through me.

Words That Cut Deeper Than Any Blades

Your words were sharper than any blade I ever faced,
Crueller than the wounds a war has traced.
Armor I wore through a thousand storms,
forged by heartbreaks, betrayals, and norms.

It held through battles; it weathered the rain,
It bore the weight of sorrow and pain.
Yet your voice, so quiet, so terribly kind,
Found every weakness I thought I left behind.

Like a knife through butter, your words slipped through,
Undoing the pieces I thought you never knew.
I was ready — at least, that's what I believed,
Armoured in lessons of all I'd received.

But nothing could make the heart ready for this fall;

No steel, no stone, no fortress at all.

I was wrong — I see it now, clear and strong —

I was not ready, and I never was.

It doesn't matter how the journey ended; what matters is–

Was it worth the pain?

Echoes from the Past

Maybe in another time, somewhere far,
A distance place beneath a brighter star;
A world where clocks drift with ease,
And laughter lingers on a soft breeze;
Or realms beyond where dreams are spun,
Where night and day blend into one;
Maybe there, we could have begun.

Where footsteps linger, slow and light,
And words unsaid take gentle flight;
A place where silence bears no pain,
And path once crossed are bound again;
Threads of light weave soft and true,
In spaces warmed by morning dew;
That's a world where I could walk with you.

Perhaps somewhere beyond the skies,

Where echoes sing and never die;

In memories neither lost nor gone,

Where endless nights give way to dawn;

In quiet reals, where hearts don't sever,

Held close by dreams that last forever;

Maybe there, you and I could be together.

Seen

I typed it slow, then hit erase,
Wrote it again—just in case.
A simple line, not much to say,
But everything I felt that day.
"Hey, just checking in," it read,
A whisper of what went unsaid.
No flood of words, no grand appeal,
Just hoping you would somehow feel.
The ticks turned blue—two silent marks,
Like distant stars in darkened parks.
You saw it there, I know you did,
But left it where the silence hid.
No typing dots, no sigh, no send,
Just space where closeness used to bend.
And though it's gone and time has passed,

I check that chat—like it might last.

Not for a reply or final clue,

But to remember *I once reached you.*

Unsent Texts

I typed your name, then hit delete,

Too many thoughts I can't repeat.

I had a line, it sounded true—

But what's the point? It's not for you.

I wrote, *"I miss the way things were,"*

But left it sitting there to blur.

It felt too late, or maybe weak—

Like wounds that heal but still don't speak.

I've got a folder full of pain,

Unsent, unread, but just the same.

They hold the words I won't confess,

The things I carry, more or less.

You'll never read the things I hide—

The parts of me I set aside.

But still, at night, my fingers bend

To write the texts that I know I'll never send.

Blocked, But Still Texting

You blocked me cold, and yet I write—
These messages, night after night.
They'll never reach your screen again,
But I still type like you're the end.
It's stupid, yeah—I know it is.
But silence hits much worse than this.
So I send thoughts into the void,
Where love once lived, now just destroyed.
"I saw that place we used to go..."
"You'd laugh at how I look now though."
I text like you might still be there,
Just reading everything, somewhere.
My phone lights up—I hope, then choke.
It's never you. It's just a joke.
I scroll up through what we once were,

Like maybe pain can make it blur.

I should delete you. I should heal.

But ghosting doesn't make it real.

You blocked me—yeah, I get the cue.

But I still text, like I'm not through.

Golden Days

Summer or winter, we'd stand together,
In drought or rain, we'd divide never.
Spring or fall, memories we'd make,
In fog or snow, our love was never fake.
Through joy and sorrow, in countless ways,
Those were our golden days.

That night, where the mountains gleamed,
By the river, where moonlight streamed.
Under the moon, where your eyes would shine,
Stars whisper secrets, while your hand in mine.
We danced through the stars, lost in a haze,
Those were our golden days.

We flew through the valleys, fearless and free,
Wandered through the alleys, just you and me.
We braved through the storms, our hearts aligned,
Chased our dreams, left our pain behind.
Clung to our hope, through love's warm blaze,
Yes, you are right, those were our golden days.

Heart vs. Mind

The mind said, *"Stop. You've bled enough."*
The heart replied, *"But love's not tough."*
One drew lines, the other wings,
One clutched facts, the other clings.
The mind recalled each sleepless night,
Each red flag waved in plain daylight.
It warned of pain, of past regrets,
Of words we wish we could forget.
But the heart—it hummed a softer song,
Of laughter shared and holding on.
It knew the cracks, it felt the fall,
Yet still believed, despite it all.
The mind builds walls, the heart breaks through,
One sees the truth, the other only *you.*
And in between, I stand and sway,

Torn by what to do... or to say.

For every time I try to choose,

I win a part, and a part I lose.

When in love, you will lose yourself,

and then slowly, painfully,

You will find pieces of yourself in places you never thought to look;

In the quiet mornings, in the cracked promises,

in the moments you thought you couldn't bear.

I stood in the ruins,

where love once lived,

tracing the edges of what was lost,

the space where you once held me close.

Your absence echoed louder than your presence,

a hollow sound I couldn't fill with anything but the silence

that followed your name.

In the wreckage,

I searched for the parts of me.

I had buried it beneath your gaze.

I found a piece of laughter,

cracked but still bright,

a sliver of dreams,

shattered but breathing.

I wasn't sure who I was without you—

or if I could even be anyone at all.

But slowly, the pieces began to shift,

like stars rearranging in a dark sky;

new constellations forming from the fragments

of who I had once been.

I relearned the taste of freedom,

and the sound of my own voice,

no longer drowned in the weight of your silence.

I learned to stand tall again,

not because I wanted to,

but because I had to.

The wounds you left behind

are now **the map of my journey**,

and **the scars**,

they're **not marks of defeat**—

they're **stories of survival**.

I rediscovered myself

in the mirror of my own reflection,

the one **I'd forgotten in the shadow of your love**.

And now, I wear my solitude

not as a burden,

but as a crown

built from the strength of my own heart,

a heart that beats again,

not for you,

but for me.

Love will teach you not just to give up, but to stand back up.

Not for them, not for anyone, but for the person you forgot to save.

And in the end,

you realize that loyalty doesn't just mean giving,

but knowing when to reclaim what's yours,

when to stop losing yourself to people who never really understood you.

You find the balance between the losses and the gains.

And finally in this journey, you learn that even in the darkest hours,

there's a kind of grace in the way we stumble forward,

as if our steps were written in a language we're yet to learn.

Although love is a beautiful thing to experience, it's also a double-edged sword.

You have to be careful.

Love someone too much, and they will end up killing your soul.

Unheard Whispers

I wrote stories, penned poems, composed a song,
But where did I go wrong?
In many tales, your name I etched,
In the only song I ever confessed.
In the poetry that I never wrote,
A silent verse still clings to my throat.
Why aren't you here? I never asked aloud,
Yet these voices, beyond my control, cried out.

Not in my stories, but in the memories, you dwell,
Not in my song, but in the music I felt.
I never wrote a poetry for you,
Yet, in every line, your absence grew.
Why aren't you here? I never asked aloud,
But in every breath, your name I vowed.

In this collection of poetry, **"Unheard Whispers"** might not be the best one, but it is something that is precious to me. It's the one that holds a corner of my heart where once you belonged.

Friendship is a strong word.

We love each other.

We share our dreams,

Our secrets, our laughter.

We lift each other.

When the world feels heavy,

We fight for one another—

Fiercely, without pause.

And yes,

Sometimes we fight with each other too.

Words slip, tempers rise,

But never for long.

Because at the end of the day,

There's no place,

That feels more like home,

Than being with you.

A friendship that blooms, soft and new,
Like morning light with skies so bright.
We talk, we laugh, we share our dreams,
Not knowing what the future means.

Unexpected Saviour

You came into my life,
Like rain in a forest fire,
Unaware, yet you saved me,
From ruin, from the pyre.
Now all I seek,
Is your presence and support,
My only desire.

Carefree Laughter

With you, I laugh and lose all care,
In games, in jokes, we're everywhere.
Laughter echoes, bright and free,
Your playful heart is home to me.
We chase the sun, we chase the moon,
Dancing through life in a carefree tune.
Every moment is a treasure found,
With you, the world spins round and round.
In mischief's glow, we roam the day,
With you beside me, come what may.
The world may change, but this remains,
Our friendship's laughter, breaking chains.

We grew up,

or maybe we just grew apart.

Messages slowed,

but you never quite left my heart.

Classroom of Memories,

Strangers, young and shy,
With curious hearts and dreams to try.
Through chalk-stained days and lunchtime cheers,
Our bond grew stronger every year.
Now sweet memories and moments true,
Are stitched with laughter shared with you.
Though time may have sent us apart,
School friends will always be in our heart.

Some days I miss you like a favourite song —

faint on the wind,

but still singing along.

You hurt me too, though I said I was fine.
I hurt you back, in ways I still can't define.
Friendship isn't always gentle or fair —
Sometimes it frays when no one is there.

Fights that Never Last

We throw our words like careless stones,
Build up our tempers, break our tones.
A flare, a frown, a slammed-back door—
We've danced this dance many times before.
You say too much, I say too loud,
We part like thunder from a cloud.
But silence never stays too long,
And hearts like ours still beat as one.
A meme, a nudge, a half-meant grin,
You text me: "Still mad?" I type, "You win."
No grudge can live where laughter grows,
And even wounds can heal, and we know.
For some may part when things go wrong,
But we've been stubborn friends for too long.
We fight like fire—but just as fast,

We're fine again, our storms don't last.

So, say your piece, I'll roll my eyes,

Then let it go like shifting skies.

Because in truth, through every test—

We break, we bend, but we don't rest.

We love too deep to let things die.

We fight, we fall, then you and I—

We find our way, the same old track.

No matter what, you're always back.

I carry us in a **pocket of time**,

pressed like a flower

between pages of rhyme.

And if you ever call,

I'll still answer the same —

with your **old nickname**,

and no traces of blame.

Bond that's Not Blood

Not bound by blood, yet still so near,

A voice I trust, a soul sincere.

You walk beside me through storm and shine,

And all your battles feel like mine.

We've laughed in rooms where joy was born,

Held each other when hearts were torn.

Shared silence deep enough to speak

What words would only make me too weak.

Through distance, time, and changing skies,

You never let the small goodbyes

Become the end. You held the thread—

The one that tied us, soul to stead.

It's not just jokes or calls at night,

But knowing when to hold on tight.

A bond that doesn't boast or bend,

The kind that says: "I'm here. My friend."

So, here's to us—no mask, no disguise,

A mirror held in honest eyes.

Whatever roads we walk, we know,

We carry one another as we go.

A Poetry for Us

You are the calm in chaos,
A hand that caught my fall.
No need for grand and practice art,
You speak the language of art.

Where others pass like passing rain,
You stay through my joy and pain.
In every laugh, in every sigh,
You paint a sun across my sky.

We've shared our dreams and silence scars,
Mapped constellations out of stars.
Though the world may twist and bend,
Our friendship will never end.

Friendship might never end.

No matter how far away we go,

No matter how hard we fight,

No matter what the situation puts us into,

Once sworn, never apart.

Bul when it ends,

It feels like a part within our soul has died.

The laughter echoes in empty halls,
Memories flicker like old film reels—
Blurry smiles, once so vivid.

No fights, no flames, just drifting seas,

A ship lost to quiet breeze.

Some stories end with no cry,

But with some footsteps, passing by.

Thank You, My Old Friend

When life was falling, I couldn't stand.,
You reached out and took my hand.
I never believed in my own might,
But you always gave me the strength to fight.

Darkness filled my world, when hope got thin,
You bought the light I needed within.
I owe you a favour that I cannot repay,
Thank you, my old friend for never turning away.

Family

Looks that need no words,
In the silence, where truths are still heard,
In the hands that hold you dear,
Where every shoulder is to dry your tear.

Love that stays when times are tough,
When what you have feels just enough,
A bond that time cannot undo,
This sacred thread, both old and new,
Stitched with care, firm and free,
This unknown strength is a family.

Family problems are something no-one is built to handle.

Even if the problems are little, they can destroy your inner peace.

Beneath the Cracks

Beneath the cracks of broken walls,
A thousand whispered burdens call,
Words unsaid, and dreams put by,
Tucked away with heavy sighs.

At dinner tables, eyes look down,
Hearts wear silence like a crown,
The fights, the tears, the shattered plates,
All stitched with love we recreate.

A mother's hands, rough from the years,
Hide her pain, dry her fears,
A father's back, bowed from the load,
Still walks a never-ending road.

Children grow with half-known tales,

Of promises made, of secret fails,

Learning early how to bend,

How sometimes love and loss are friends.

A Family isn't Always Light

We build our lives from pieces torn,
From sacrifice, from dreams forlorn,
And still we choose, again and again,
To hold the weight, to bear the rain.

For blood is more than perfect days,
It's in the mess, the fight, the fray,
It's in the choosing not to run,
The staying, when the pain is not done.

Family isn't always light,
It's scars that speak, it's endless nights,
It's love that bleeds, then stands once more,
A battered ship returning to shore.

Together but Not

We live under the same roof,
But not together.
Family is supposed to be made of love,
Yet responsibilities are the only thing left here.

Where we failed and all went wrong, I wonder,
Beneath this fancy light, we used to laugh together.
As time flies by, our words disappear,
Those dinner-time tales, ended forever.

"How was your day?"
Nobody cares.
"This has to be done"
That's all they speak to each other.

No matter how much I sacrificed,

No matter how hard I tried,

It seems they were never satisfied.

Never Enough

I sacrificed my childhood for your dreams,
Traded laughter for silence and sunbeams.
Gave up my hopes just to see you smile,
Walked in your shadow mile after mile.
I stitched your pride into every thread,
While letting mine quietly fall dead.
You reached for more with greedy hands,
While I built castles from sinking sands.
My voice grew hoarse from silent cries,
But you just chased the next disguise.
No "thank you", no glance behind,
Just hunger dressed in love, that's unkind.
Now I stand, empty, worn and wise,
The child you lost behind your lies.
And still you ask for something new—
But I have nothing left to give to you.

I've watched your eyes drift far away, though you smile and nod,
As if you're praying silently, still placing your faith in God.

You whispered prayers beneath your breath, while I just watch and wait,
Unsure if love still lights your path, or if I came too late.

You built a world with your hands and hope carved deep in your bone,

While I chased the fleeting shadows, scared to walk the path you had once shown.

You taught me strength in silence, in the way you never cried,

But I hear the sadness in your voice whenever you say, “I’m fine” and lied.

I failed not just in action, but in the heart that wouldn't strive,

To rise above my comfort and give you reasons to feel alive.

You gave your best so I could shine, yet here I stand still in fear,

With promises that fade like stars, as morning draws near.

You try to understand this road I chose to trend,
But I know you wonder quietly if I've been misled.
I hear it in the questions that are simple yet profound,
Like "Are you eating?" "Sleeping?" – Just trying to hold me while I drown.

Son that I Couldn't Become

I should have been the son you speak of with a burning pride,

But I'm the one you pray for, when the night won't let you hide.

The one who said, "I'll make it," but keeps falling short again and again,

Leaving footprints made of doubt and a trail of silent pain.

Maybe Someday

I swear one day I'll come to you, with something in my hands,
Not riches, not grand titles, but a life that understands.
What it means to make you proud, to finally let you see,
That every dream you gave to me still lives and breathes within me.

And if I fail a thousand times, I'll still get up and try,
Because no man is truly broken who still makes his father cry.
Not with grief or disappointment, but with tears of honest grace,
For knowing that his son came home, and found his rightful place.

This book, **"Love, Friendship and Them"** means a lot to me. For me, it's not just a book, it's a message to the people I love and care about.

But for them, it's nothing.

Cigarettes that I Burn

The smoke curls like a whispered lie,
Dancing through shadows I try to deny.
Each spark a moment I can't forget,
Each ash a promise drowned in regret.

They say flames dies, but never the ache,
And silence is louder with every intake.
So, I light another, not for the thrill,
But to quiet the ghosts that I know I never will.

Conclusion

I spent hours thinking about why my life is messed up from all sides.

After countless hours of silence, it hit me— It finally started to make sense, why do people keep leaving me behind in the dust?

The problem is not them, not the world around me.

It's me, it was always me.

I failed –

as a lover,

as a partner,

as a friend,

as a brother,

and worst of all,

I failed as a son.

To the one who read with their heart,

Who paused at pain,

Who smiled at softness—

This book was my silence.

You made it a voice.

Thank you.

And yet... I still have more to say